What Drives You?

How Our Family Dynamics Shape the People We Become

Ellen Yashinsky Chute

Contents

To my children, Julie, Amy, and Danny. Being a part of your journeys has been the most important thing in my life.

And to my husband, Paul, who won't give up on me, even when I want to give up on myself.

Introduction

I grew up as an only child without an extended family or large social group around me. The experience that encapsulated how it felt being me in my family was sitting alone in the back seat of our family car while my parents interacted with each other up front. I thought of myself as the little girl alone in the back seat. It wasn't sad or lonely; it was just my lived experience.

As I grew up, I had a strong drive to connect with people and made many friends. I spent time with my friends' families and found that they were different from mine. They were interactive, louder, more intense. They had more people.

I was keenly interested in these noisy, engaged groups of people and how they shaped the individuals in them. Those childhood interests and observations were part of what eventually led me to social work and teaching.

At the University of Michigan School of Social Work, I taught beginning social workers how to work with families. To illustrate how family dynamics shaped us, I drew from my own experiences in my family car. I set up four chairs at the front of the room to represent a car and sat in the back seat. I described my parents in the front seat and asked my students how they thought I felt back there and how it might have shaped my view of myself and the world.

Teaching this concept at the beginning of the class gave my students a way to envision how they might be helpful to the families they might work with. It also helped them understand their own histories and become aware of what they learned about themselves in their own cars, which is valuable knowledge for anybody who is working with families.

So many students would tell me, "Oh my gosh, I called my mom as soon as I left your class," or "I just had to call my brother to talk about this." It provided a lot of "aha" moments for my students.

It also provided a lot of "aha" moments in my practice. I was recently working with a woman whose father was in cognitive decline. She was angry because she was organizing his care and her siblings were only pitching in when she told them what to do. I explained the car metaphor to her and pointed out that her father used to be in the driver's seat but was no longer able to fill that role. Neither she nor her siblings wanted to be the driver, but in her already established role as "family caretaker," she had reluctantly assumed the role.

Nothing in her life prepared her for it. As for so many of my clients, explaining those dynamics in terms of everyone's seat in the car illuminated her family's changing and challenging interactions in a way that helped her see the situation and her own behavior and reactions more clearly. This book, *What Drives You?*, was written to help you have that same "aha" moment.

In these pages, you will find easy-to-read explanations of how we develop as children, how we adopt roles in our families, and how we carry those roles into our adult lives. Each chapter includes questions to guide you as you examine your family car and the lessons you learned in it.

Understanding how we became the people we are and what drives us can help us improve our mental health, our relationships, our professional lives, and, perhaps most importantly, the families we create.

Although it can be challenging to revisit certain childhood experiences, my hope for you is that looking at yours will help you find compassion for yourself as an adult, for the child you once were, and for all the other people in your life.

1
How Is a Family Like a Car?

We each have our own family story. Each of our stories is made up of memories and impressions, along with our understanding of childhood events and interactions. Those stories largely shape how we see ourselves and how we interact with others.

I have one, too. This, in a very small nutshell, is my family story:

My mother was an only child. She was born to a wholesale produce vendor and his wife in a small town outside Pittsburgh in 1921. Although her family went through the Depression, my mother had food and suffered relatively little from the experience. She did, however, suffer at the hands of my grandmother, who was severely mentally ill and brutally critical. Nothing was ever good enough for her, and my mother grew up desperate to escape.

Both highly intelligent and absolutely determined, my mother was admitted to a top university at age 17, which was very unusual for a young woman in 1938.

While she was studying for a Bachelor of Fine Arts in dress design, she met my father, a young engineering student, fell in love, and got married. After my father graduated, he went to war and my mother moved to Baltimore, supporting the war effort through a job at the Army's Aberdeen Proving Grounds.

After the war, my father got a job in Detroit and moved there with my mother. When I was 18 months old, they divorced, and my mother started dating a young man in their social circle. My father left, remarried, and moved to another state with his new wife and her daughter, who was exactly my age, before having two more daughters.

I saw my father and his new family infrequently until I was four and then not at all for many years. He later told me he left believing I would have a family with my mother and her boyfriend. In those days, it was common for children of divorce not to have equal time with both parents. My mother's boyfriend became a fixture in my life for several years, but because he was hesitant to commit to marriage, my mother finally ended their relationship and moved us to California, tearing me away from another key person in my life.

As an adult, I understand the impact this chain of losses had on me. My story is that I had family, and I lost them; I got new sisters, and I lost them. These losses were significant events that shaped me in many ways.

One day, my mother told me we were expecting an exciting surprise in two weeks. Throughout my childhood, she had always used her fashion skills to make me beautiful clothes, and for this special occasion, she made me a pastel blue waisted dress with a full skirt, a white organza pinafore, and a bolero. It was very special, but it pinched and constrained me, as the beautiful clothes she made me often did. I learned when I was very young that looking good was much more important to my mother than comfort.

The day of the surprise came. It was time for me to put the new dress on, make sure the bow was straight in the back and my anklets were straight in my Mary Janes, and prepare to be a good girl. We went to the Beverly Hills Hotel. There were doormen and many ladies who were dressed up. Everyone looked so fancy, and I rechecked my bow and anklets to make sure I looked perfect.

We took the elevator up and when the doors opened, there was my mother's boyfriend, who swooped me up and swung me around. I was so glad to see him. It was a perfect, beautiful day: there was our reunion and the glamorous setting, but the icing on the cake was that I was served a huge strawberry on a fancy silver dish. It was at least four inches across, and I had never seen anything like it. I could feel my eyes widen looking at this one big perfect strawberry, laid in front of me like a present.

After lunch, a friend of my mother's came to our house. My mother said her friend was going to stay with me for a few days while she went away. With that, my mother and her boyfriend went to Las Vegas, got married, then came back to quickly pack up all our stuff and move us all back to Michigan.

That's a little bit of my childhood story. As I said, we all have one—and understanding mine has greatly helped me understand myself as an adult.

If we use the car as a metaphor for a family, we can imagine that when I was born, my father was in the driver's seat, my mother was in the front passenger seat, and I was in the back seat. This seating arrangement lasted for 18 months. When my birth father left the car and my mother took the driver's seat, I moved into the front passenger seat, as happens often for an only child with a single parent. At the age of seven, my new father took over the driver's seat, my mother went back to the passenger seat, and I was in the back seat again.

Returning to the back seat was lonely for me, especially after being in the front seat for six years while my mother was single. I remained in the back seat throughout my childhood and adolescence.

As a baby, the unexplained early loss of my father must have been terrifying. As young children often do, I likely assumed that his absence was my fault somehow and wanted to do whatever I could to ensure that I didn't lose another person who was close to me, which meant following the rules in our car. I know from what I have learned as an adult and as a social worker that when a child loses a parent, they work really hard to hold onto the one they have. My way of holding onto my mother was to take care of her, and that became my role in our family.

When I was 40, I went into therapy. In the intake session, I told the therapist I was an only child. After I told the rest of the story, she said, "You're not an only child. You have a stepsister and two half-sisters." As much as I would have given anything for a bigger family, I was so uncomfortable—my entire identity was that I was an only child. After taking some time to assimilate this new understanding of my family, I found my birth father's address and wrote him a letter telling him that I'd like to be in touch with him. He wrote me back a 12-page letter saying he and his wife would love to see me, and I went to meet them.

When I arrived, my father was babysitting his three-year-old grandchild. He was so warm and open and deeply happy to see me. I felt like I was a gift to him. We sat at the table in his kitchen and caught up on each other's lives. After an hour, his wife came in, threw her arms around me and said, "We wanted you so badly, but your mother just wouldn't allow it. We thought it was best for you if we didn't push it."

At the time, my marriage was faltering, and we ultimately divorced. I found myself in the driver's seat for the first time in my life. Before then, my role had always been to make the person in the driver's seat comfortable. I struggled to adjust to my new place in my car. It was our family therapist who helped me learn how to help my children develop the skills they needed to succeed in life by setting appropriate boundaries and limits for them, rather than catering to my own need to keep everyone happy.

As we'll see in more detail in Chapter 3: Roles and Rules in the Family Car, all families have spoken and unspoken rules. In our family, the spoken rule was "little girls are to be seen and not heard." I took it literally and tried my best to adhere. The unspoken rules in our family were that I should *be good, look pretty, and have minimal needs.*

These behaviors became my default responses to life. In our families, we interact constantly, and those interactions affect us like a groove that gets worn into a floor where there's a lot of traffic. Our regular behavior, our default behaviors, get repeated over and over, and because of the sheer number of repeated interactions, these responses are stored in our brains and bodies and become our identities.

As a result of my own repeated interactions, I avoid confrontation. I minimize my needs. I try to be helpful. I have a hard time asking for help, so I've learned to take care of things myself. My loneliness in the back seat also drove me to seek connection with others, to feel like I mattered to them; other people with similar beginnings might develop different default behaviors. For some, early losses cause distance and disconnection in their families, and they carry those tendencies forward in their lives.

In this book, I explain these dynamics in more detail. As you're reading, if you think about your own default behaviors as an adult, you will likely see the influences of your family, its rules and your own role in it.

The concept of the "family car" is a unique way to understand the powerful influences our family systems exert on our development. That understanding helps me have compassion for myself when it is hard to have a voice, or when I struggle with asking for help. As I've seen firsthand, my students have benefited from this unique way of understanding themselves and their clients. In my work with individuals and families, I have also used it to help people develop a compassionate understanding of how they became the people they are and why they do the things they do.

I wrote this book because I believe that families have the power to promote powerful positive change in the world. When a child grows up in a family that helps them feel worthy and lovable despite their trials and tribulations, they are able to overcome life's obstacles and discover their true strength. When we feel okay about ourselves as adults, we are able to act toward the common good.

When children grow up feeling as though they are disappointments and undeserving, they expend their life's energy trying to feel important or proving to themselves that they matter, or that they are enough. When we don't know that we are enough, our actions are directed toward looking for the validation we didn't receive as children, rather than toward the common good.

The goal of this book is to help people understand how they developed into the individuals they are, to be able to accept that with compassion, and to understand that we do the best we can with what we've been given. We all have stories that explain how we understand our families and our childhoods, and as adults, we can look at them and get a better understanding of the events and dynamics that affected us. In turn, we can understand our own actions with compassion for the younger people we once were.

Some of what you read here may bring up memories and feelings that are challenging. I encourage you to approach this process with great kindness toward yourself—both for the person you are now and the person who lived these experiences.

If you are a parent, the power to help yourself and the members of your family feel worthy, important, and lovable is available to everyone. If you didn't get enough of this in your own childhood, it might not come naturally to you, but it can come intentionally. This book will help you to understand how to do this. You deserve it, your families deserve it, and the world needs it.

2
What Is a Family?

It's 1974. A green station wagon is traveling north, carrying a family to a ski vacation. In the front, Harvey, the father, is driving, and his wife, Sally, is sitting in the passenger seat; when they are together, he always drives. She has brought a bag of snacks. She passes Cheez-Its and grapes to their three children, Ann, Charlie, and Ricky, on request.

In the way back of the station wagon, the seats are folded down and Ann and her two brothers lay in their sleeping bags (because this was before seat belts were required), trying to tune a show in on a portable black and white television. The signal is fading and after a couple of hours they are out of range. Ann is 12 and her brothers are nine and seven. Since she's the oldest, she has control of the TV and keeps trying the tuning knob to see if she can get something other than static.

It begins to rain. Water starts to trickle in through the leaky gasket surrounding the back window—first as little drips and then rivulets, running down the window, over the green vinyl inside the door, and, finally, onto the sleeping bags.

Ricky, who will eventually become an engineer, grabs a box of tissues, starts wadding them up, and shoves the wads into the hole in the gasket. Charlie, the youngest and "the smart one," pulls his feet away from the growing damp and quietly continues working on a detailed drawing of a Grumman F6F Hellcat he saw in one of their father's WWII books. Ann shuts off the now-useless TV and begins wadding and stuffing tissues as well.

"Hey, this was my idea," objects Rick, elbowing her.

"I want to do it too," says Ann, reaching for the box of tissues as Ricky holds them out of her reach. "I want a turn."

They start shoving each other in the tight space and their father shouts, "Ann, stop it!"

Ann cries, "It's not my fault! It's Rick. He's hogging the tissue box."

"You're the oldest," her father calls back. "You make it work."

The Family Car

While you were reading that story, chances are you had a vivid image of your own childhood car: the people in the car, where you were sitting, where everyone else was sitting; who was talking, who was quiet; who demanded potty stops; who complained that someone else was touching them or snapping their gum or making annoying noises; who farted for fun, and who turned their face out the window to daydream, and who tried to start a word game or a round of singing; who decided where you were going; who was driving; how it felt to be you in that car and how you felt about the others.

The family car is a place where we're physically close to each other, a place where we're almost forced to interact. It's a microcosm of the dynamics in our family, a distillation of the delicate dance of everyone's personalities, desires, and developmental stages.

It's also a great metaphor for the family.

What Is a Family?

The purpose of a family, in purely scientific terms, is to protect small humans until they can take care of themselves and to prepare them to do so.

But we all know that families do much more than simply keeping junior from walking into traffic or tasting the cleaning supplies. That's because keeping children safe and helping them grow into self-sufficient adults also means providing a safe place for them to develop mentally, emotionally, and socially.

A family is not a group of individuals living their own separate lives. It is a group of people who feel connected to one another, who move through time together, and whose relationships form an interconnected system. When a family works well, it grows and evolves as the individual members learn, develop, and interact, becoming the best expressions of who they are.

Well-functioning families help children grow into adults who can:

- Take risks
- Rebound from failures
- Express emotions (rather than act them out in ways that keep them from their goals)
- Have a reasonable amount of trust for other human beings
- Have a general sense that they control the outcomes in their lives
- Build a satisfying life
- Experience joy

How Is a Family Like a Car?

To understand how a family works, it might help to think of it as a machine with interconnected parts that move together, driving each other. In this book, we look at the family system as a car because in our families, we travel together, both through time and toward the goals we have for ourselves as individuals and as a group. The car's job is to get the family members from today to tomorrow and the next day.

In our cars, we each have unique and equally important roles to play to keep the car going.

Family cars, at their best, are well-oiled machines that work in ways that support the development of all their members as they travel down the road.

In this book, we're going to take a look at different kinds of cars, our roles in our cars, and how this understanding can empower us in our adult lives and help us build cars that will help our children grow into healthy adults. At the end of each chapter, you'll find some questions designed to help you understand your family car and your seat in it. There are no right or wrong answers to these questions. They are designed to help you think about and understand your childhood family experience.

Looking Back with an Adult Brain

To understand your role in your family, you'll need to travel backwards in time to the years you spent in your family car. If you have difficult memories, it may be painful, but using this book as a guide, you may find yourself gaining different and valuable insights into your family dynamics and childhood events by looking at them from an adult point of view.

Why will your memories look different now? It's not just that you're older and wiser. It's also that your brain is quite different than it was when you were a child. Just like the rest of our bodies, our brains change as we grow from birth to adulthood. Our brains are not fully formed when we are born. As we grow, they grow, making new connections and developing new abilities to think, experience emotion, create memories, understand others, plan, and make decisions.

As our brains and bodies develop, the way we think and understand develops, too. As a result, we process what's happening in our lives and with our families differently at different times in our life.

The Developing Brain

The brain develops from infancy to young adulthood, with different parts becoming fully functional at different stages. Understanding how the brain develops can help us look back on our childhood selves with more compassion and parent in a way that supports the development of our children through each stage. Let's take a look at what these parts of the brain do and when they develop.

1. Birth Through Early Childhood

At birth, the part of our brain that is fully developed is the brain stem or the reptilian brain. It controls our heart rate, breathing, balance, movement, body temperature, and sleep, as well as our fight, flight, or freeze response.

During this time in our lives, our brains are focused on survival. Babies need food, sleep, comfort and human touch to survive. Although it may seem otherwise, babies only cry because they need one of these things.

Until about age six, we are in a stage of ego-centric thinking, meaning we think everything that happens is about us. When mommy or daddy are in a bad mood, we think we did something to cause that. It's at this stage that we form ideas that aren't necessarily true about how lovable we are and how much we matter. In the young mind, what this may sound like is:

Mommy and daddy are fighting. It's my fault. That means I'm bad and not worthy.

Most parents don't know this is how their children make sense of things, so they often aren't aware that they need to contradict the false ideas that can appear in a child's mind. They don't know their child might be developing ideas that aren't necessarily true about events in the family and that it might be really important for that child to talk to them about their feelings.

The untrue beliefs we develop about ourselves and the world at this early age due to our ego-centric thinking stay with us forever, or until something in our life offers us enough evidence to begin contradicting them. Ego-centric thinking causes us to make assumptions about the world and our own worth and value that are untrue, and those assumptions have a physical effect on our brain's development. They become part of our wiring, and we take them with us on our life journey.

2. Adolescence

Adolescents go through a burst of brain development that affects all aspects of their physical and mental functioning. In adolescence, the limbic part of our brains become fully developed. The limbic part of the brain controls memory, emotions, hormones, mood, motivation, and the pain and pleasure response.

This part of the brain is really fired up during adolescence, with a flood of sex hormones suddenly affecting mood and excitability. This is why adolescents are so emotional, and why we see so much adolescent anxiety and depression. Because there is so much going on in their developing brains, it takes high-intensity activities to trigger the limbic system's reward circuits.

Unfortunately, because their brains are not fully developed, they cannot yet consider the consequences of their actions, be thoughtful in their decision-making or become proficient in other executive functions like flexible thinking, self-control and empathy, which often don't develop until the pre-frontal cortex is fully formed in our early 20s.

This is why we may shudder when we think back to our own adolescence and some of the ill-considered choices we made.

3. Early Adulthood

In our mid-20s, the final piece falls into place as the pre-frontal cortex comes fully online, controlling abstract thought, planning, and our ability to understand consequences. As this happens, our ability to understand life through someone else's eyes increases, and our ability to feel empathy for others is enhanced. Our brain becomes fully functional, meaning that we gain much greater control over tasks such as impulse control, planning, and decision-making. This additional brain functionality also allows us to gain a different perspective and a more complex understanding of our experiences.

Driving Down Memory Lane with Your Adult Brain

The way we understand the events in our lives and our family relationships is different at each stage of our development. The age we are when an event happens determines how we understand it, and that is how we will remember and understand it until we revisit it with our more complex adult brain.

This means that how we understand family memories can change over time. Revisiting an event from your teenage years may give you an "aha!" moment of clarity as your adult brain reprocesses your actions and the actions of those involved. You may see everyone's behavior differently, understand motives and reactions much better, and realize that your own behavior was driven by a brain that was not finished developing.

Your fully-developed brain understands events that happened in your past with much more clarity and complexity than your younger brain did at the time.

As adults, we can:

- Observe ourselves as children
- Feel compassion for our younger selves
- Understand our own development and that of our family members
- Understand the complex dynamics of our families

With this better understanding, we start to realize that some of our current behavior may be a result of beliefs and patterns created by our younger brains. Our adult brains can update these patterns to work better for us in our adult lives.

Ned Was the Center of a Weird Universe

Ned's parents divorced when he was five. When it happened, he was at the stage of brain development where he believed that if something bad happened, he had caused it. So, he believed he caused his parents' divorce. He believed it was his fault and he always thought he was bad because of that, but without consciously understanding that this belief came from egocentric thinking. When he revisited that memory as an adult, he would still experience it from a child's point of view, and it was very painful. He would shudder, change the subject, or have a physical reaction like a stomachache or tight neck that indicated those feelings were still in there and still hurt the same way they did when it happened.

Because his view of himself and his life continued to be based on the understanding of his five-year-old self, his actions as an adult were based on that perspective as well. He felt he wasn't good enough, that he was from a "weird" family, that other people had "normal" families and he didn't. He internalized the badness he felt as a child and carried it with him into adulthood.

When we experience events like divorce at a young age, we tend to make general assumptions about them. Without enough context, clarifying information, or brain development, we often come away believing that they are indicative of who we are or who our family is. Then we make assumptions that other people and other families are normal and perfect, and we may feel less-than, inadequate, or not good enough.

If we go into adulthood with these beliefs, we may believe we are:

- **Unlovable, not worthy of love, or unattractive**.
  We may feel uncomfortable getting our physical and

14

emotional needs met for affection, sex, and human contact because we feel defective.

- **Unimportant, or not valuable**. We may feel that we don't matter, that we're not respected, or that no one cares what we have to say. We may feel that nobody notices us.
- **Inadequate**. We may feel that we're not "enough" in some way, that we lack some important quality. For example, we might feel we're not thin, smart, classy, tough, or manly enough.
- **Undeserving**. If we're raised in an environment that feels critical and punishing, we may not realize that we can make life better for ourselves. We don't do the things we've always wanted to do because we don't feel that we are entitled to them. So, we settle for unhealthy relationships or don't go after jobs we'd like.

When we feel this way, we're likely to respond in one of two very different ways. We may try to:

- **Confirm the belief**. We may act in ways that prove that our belief is true. If we feel we are unlovable, we may act in unlovable ways; if we feel we are undeserving, we may decline opportunities for activities we'd enjoy.
- **Try to dispute the belief**. If the belief is that we are "less than," for example, we may try to rack up professional accomplishments or material wealth that proves otherwise.

What Arlene Learned

Arlene's father was somewhat distant and emotionless, and Arlene repeatedly felt rejected by him. Her mother was loud and brash, and Arlene found her intimidating. As a result, she became extremely introverted and genuinely scared of people. She didn't understand that other people were not like her father. As a result of

15

the understanding she developed as a child, she never gave herself a chance to be open and connect with people.

One of the most important things for a child to feel in their home is that they are a delight to their parents, and Arlene didn't get that. So, Arlene assumed that she was not lovable, that she didn't matter and wasn't important.

As a child, she couldn't understand that her self-perception was just about her father's behavior. She would strive to fade into the background and stay out of any spotlight. In high school, she almost failed a public speaking class because it was so uncomfortable for her to have people look at her and watch her. She expected them to criticize and reject her. She chose friends who were also timid and quiet and avoided popular people at school and work. She chose a research job where she didn't have to interact with people much.

Relationships were extremely hard because she never learned to connect with others. Each time she met someone she liked, she would bail out at the first rough patch because she expected the relationship, like the one with her father, to end up being disconnected and unsatisfying.

She didn't know that what she had learned about people was incorrect. Not everyone acted like her father. And she never understood that her behavior was a response to that incorrect learning.

In her car, Arlene was the shy one, the introvert, the one who wasn't friendly. In time, that became the way she was seen and her identity in her family, constantly reinforced by how she was treated, how family members reacted towards her, and how people spoke to and about her. Her mom often apologized for her at family gatherings, saying, "Don't take it personally—Arlene's just very shy." This became her identity, the way she saw herself, and she carried this understanding of herself into adulthood.

This was very limiting in Arlene's adult life. She didn't understand that there was more to her than that, but no one around her understood that this would be helpful for her to know, so no one thought to tell her. Her family members were not bad people. But, within their family car, they reinforced that this was who she was and didn't encourage her to expand her view of herself.

As adults, we often live with these labels until we begin to understand the family dynamics that shaped how we see ourselves.

Seeing Herself Differently

The pre-frontal cortex is the part of our brain that comes online in our late teens and 20s. With it, you are able to reexamine your family and your role in it. You can also feel compassion for yourself as a child.

By using her adult brain to revisit her childhood in therapy, Arlene was able to look at herself as a child and understand the family dynamics that shaped her understanding of herself and her behavior with other people. She learned that growing up with her parents made her feel that way, and she came to understand and believe she could have different types of experiences with different people. This led her to make behavioral changes that created new and different dynamics in her relationships.

She learned that she often did things that were worth noting, and she learned to let people pay attention to her without expecting it to be unpleasant. She still preferred to be out of the spotlight, but she knew she could tolerate the spotlight when necessary. Most importantly, she learned that her contributions to the world were valuable.

When she met her boyfriend Jeff, instead of self-sabotaging, she learned to tolerate some bad times and keep going. When they had disagreements, she was able to express her feelings and have a conversation instead of withdrawing, because she had changed her belief that it was never going to work out anyway.

Becoming Unique Individuals

So, that's our individual development. While we're learning and growing, so are all the other people in our car. Each of us plays a different role and gets assigned different "identities" within our family. These come from a combination of:

- Natural inclination
- Roles modeled by our parents
- Each person's need to forge a unique identity
- The car's need to have a variety of functions filled in order to keep moving forward

As it relates to Arlene's story, Arlene's older sister Angela, for example, is extremely gregarious. As mentioned, Arlene's mother was a tough cookie, a loud and exuberant person. To Arlene, her mother's voice was daunting, and her father seemed softer and more approachable. Even though he was disconnected, it seemed easier for Arlene to model her behavior after his. Angela, on the other hand, modeled herself after her mother.

A car has a lot of parts, among them an engine, wheels, a steering wheel, and so on. All the parts, though quite different, work together to keep the car going. A family works the same way, with each person assigned certain tasks that keep the car going.

Each child born into a family will begin to seek a unique identity. Sometimes, in order to get the attention they need, a child may find an identity the family sees as negative, like "the drama queen," "the annoying one," or "the needy one." Our amazing intuition helps us choose a role that is not already taken, and which contributes to the family in a way no one else does. In a well-functioning family, our uniqueness helps us feel loved and valuable, and it allows us to contribute to how the family works in a unique way.

As important as it is for us as individuals to have a unique identity, it is equally important to the family that we fulfill our role there. Just as every part of a car does its job to keep the car running, each member of the family plays a role that keeps the family going.

When it is balanced and all the parts are operating together, the family is in a state called *homeostasis*. That means that all the interdependent parts are working together, creating stability for the car. When everyone in the car has a different role and we each play our role, the "car" will go. Homeostasis is comfortable. It helps people know what to expect and what they're supposed to do. To that end, family members tend to work hard to keep each other playing their respective roles to keep the car going.

But what happens if a family member changes their behavior?

Maybe you're the funny one everyone relies on to break the tension between parents who don't get along. What happens if you go away to college? Maybe someone in the family drinks or uses drugs and the rest of the family's function is to help them—what happens if they enter recovery? The homeostasis is broken.

The members of the family are interdependent, playing roles that contribute to keeping the car balanced and moving. In families where someone is drinking or using drugs, the roles of the other family members depended on the user continuing to use. Now each person's role must shift, which challenges the homeostasis.

Challenges to the homeostasis happen regularly in families. Any time a child is born or a grandparent moves in, or there is any significant change to who is in the car or how they're fulfilling their role, the family must reorganize, adjust, and create a new homeostasis.

Changes in homeostasis are a normal part of family development, and healthy families are able to adjust to a new homeostasis. Still, changes in a family can also be extremely uncomfortable, so it's possible that even if a member with substance use issues, for example, overcomes them, the family will continue to treat them as they did when they were using drugs or alcohol in an effort to avoid change. The family might continue to see them as needy or untrustworthy, not embracing the new strengths they've developed in recovery.

While the above example makes the process seem very obvious, in many situations, the way family members keep one another in their respective roles is much subtler. We often don't know what role we play in our families, making them ever more complex and difficult to define. Even so, those roles are the identities we bring into the world with us as adults. Understanding them helps us navigate our own thoughts and behaviors and makes sure we're behaving in ways that help us build the lives we want.

Now, Let's Look at You and Your Family

I'm writing this book because it's important to me that you know that as an adult, you can have a better understanding of your own experience and become more intentional in your thoughts and behaviors—anyone can do this.

Once you examine the forces that shaped your understanding of the world and your behavior, you get to try to change your old habits. It's a process, a practice, and a journey. It's not a straight line, and it requires us to change not only internally, but in our relationships. To change successfully, we need to reexamine how we interpret others' actions and adjust how we react based on our new insights.

The therapeutic relationship is a good place to do this. In my own practice, I help people develop these insights and behavioral changes through psychotherapy. Going through this process actually changes how our brains work, helping to reshape not just the ideas we have, but the brain that creates them. Through this relationship, we can often change how we behave in other relationships, including the ones in our families.

A book is not a replacement for therapy, but through this guide, you can begin to see your family car a little more clearly. Here are some questions you can ask yourself to get started.

———

Ask Yourself

The following questions can help you begin to look at your childhood car through adult eyes. If you think of your family as a car:

1. Where was each person sitting?
2. Who was in the driver's seat (this could be more than one person at different times)?
3. What makes you say that?
4. Where did you sit?

Think about the roles each member of your family played (from your point of view—everyone in the car may see their role differently). Was someone in the car the funny one? The obnoxious one? The quiet one, the needy one, the one who was tuned out? The one who knew everything? The over-achiever or the under-achiever? With that in mind:

1. What do you think the role of each person in your car was?
2. What was your role in your family?
3. Did you have a label? If so, what was it? "I was the _____ one."
4. Describe the roles and labels of the other members of your family.
5. In what ways do you still conform to your family role?
6. In what ways did you or do you intentionally choose not to?
7. If you created your own family as an adult, what are the roles of each member there?

Notes

3
Rules and Roles in the Family Car

It's 5:38 pm. Lisa jumps out of her car and rushes into school to pick up Charlie from aftercare. She walks into the classroom, signs the pick-up sheet and scans the room for her son. Charlie's sitting on the floor in the far corner, with his forehead pressed against the painted cinder block.

Lisa's stomach sinks. *A bad day*, she thinks, walking over to him.

"Hi, bud," she says, crouching down next to him and putting her hand on his back. Charlie stiffens and flexes his shoulder, as if to throw off her hand.

"Want to talk about it?"

Charlie looks at her sullenly, jams his arms into the sleeves of his jacket, yanks his backpack off the floor, and stomps out the door toward the car.

Lisa texts her husband Derrick: *Bad day*.

Derrick texts back: *Did he say anything?*

Lisa responds: *Nope, silence and stomping.*

A moment later: *Ugh.* And then: *Poor little guy.*

She climbs behind the wheel and turns to Charlie, who has buckled his seat belt and is hugging his Teenage Mutant Ninja Turtles backpack.

"Was it math?" She asks him—but she already knows the answer.

"I hate math," says Charlie, almost under his breath.

"I know, honey, I know," Lisa says, thinking, *damn that Mrs. Turner.* "Sounds like you're pretty frustrated."

"I hate it!"

Mrs. Turner is what Lisa generously thinks of as "old school," which means she treats Charlie as if he doesn't understand the words or isn't trying hard enough, rather than understanding that Charlie will never understand concepts such as bigger and smaller numbers as easily as his peers. He can't hold numbers in his head and doesn't get that five and 5 are the same thing.

When they sit at home and work on it, Derrick will keep giving Charlie problems and walking him patiently through them until Charlie gets it, and then it's high fives and hugs. Mrs. Turner just talks louder and louder the longer Charlie doesn't get it. Charlie feels like she's angry. Her impatience makes it harder for him to think, and the kids in his class laugh at him. That's what boils Lisa's blood the most: that Mrs. Turner doesn't get how much she's humiliating Charlie.

Lisa and Derrick have met with her, with the principal, and with the school social worker, all trying to get her to understand the problem, which is called dyscalculia. It seems to Lisa that Mrs. Turner is less capable of understanding learning disabilities than Charlie is of grasping numbers.

At a red light, she glances at her phone. Derrick texts: *BTW, Lionel scored three goals at soccer today. He's over the moon.*

"Hey, Charlie," says Lisa. "It's been a while since we had ice cream for dessert. Should we stop at the market?"

Lisa lets Charlie pick the ice cream, and he chooses moose

tracks. She knows it's not his brother's favorite, but she's hoping to lift Charlie's mood a little before he has to go home to Lionel recapping his soccer triumph and then slog through frustrating math homework.

It's been a long day and it's an easy fix, she thinks, even if she's teaching her kids to self-soothe with food and setting herself up for Lionel to grouch at her because Charlie got to pick the ice cream.

Becoming Who We Are

A well-functioning family car has space for each person to grow into the best version of their own authentic self. The people in the car both tolerate and encourage the discovery and expression of that authenticity. This means the parents are open to hearing their children and have the courage to help figure out what is genuinely best for them, even or especially in the face of challenging ideas and needs.

———

After dinner, Derrick says, "Hey, Charlie, help me get the bowls and spoons for ice cream?"

As they get up to go in the kitchen, Lisa braces herself, thinking, *I'm so tired. I don't know if I can deal with one more upset.*

Lionel says, "Oh yeah! Ice cream? What kind?"

"Moose tracks," says Lisa, watching Lionel's face immediately fall.

"Oh, man. I hate moose tracks."

"I know it's not your favorite and you're disappointed, but you can pick next time."

"Fine," says Lionel sullenly, "but this stinks."

Derrick and Charlie come back in with the ice cream, bowls, and spoons.

"Oh, we won't need four bowls," says Lisa. "Lionel *hates* moose tracks."

"No, no, I'll have some," says Lionel quickly, looking at Lisa, "but next time we can have mint chocolate chip, right, Mom?"

"Mint chocolate chip? I thought you liked birthday cake ice cream."

"When I was a little kid," says Lionel.

"Well, okay, big guy," says Derrick, scooping ice cream.

———

All children should have space to come up with all kinds of thoughts and feelings their parents never considered before—and whether it's about ice cream flavors or career interests, they deserve to be heard, acknowledged, and supported.

When children feel heard, acknowledged, and supported enough of the time, they develop an ability to tolerate uncomfortable feelings without having to act on them. A child who has a hard time in school and is disruptive in the classroom acts that way because they are having a hard time managing their feelings.

The goal of a parent is to help their children identify their emotions and learn to tolerate the discomfort. If the parent can validate the discomfort, the child won't have to act on the emotion. Let's take, for example, the parent whose child is crying at the grocery checkout because they see a piece of candy and they want it. If the parent says, "I know you want it and it would be delicious, but it's too close to dinner, so we're not going to have candy right now," the child will feel validated and be more likely to stop crying.

The child who learns to tolerate emotional discomfort can act from their thoughts instead. That means instead of lashing out or shutting down in response to feelings, they express them in words. When we act from our thoughts, we think through our decisions and then behave in a strategic, goal-directed way, rather than a reactive, emotionally driven way.

If you walk through the halls of a school and stand outside each classroom for a bit, you can often tell which teachers are operating thoughtfully and which are operating from their emotions. If a couple of kids are driving a teacher crazy, the teacher's emotional response might be to yell at them, punish them, shut down, allow chaos to erupt, or become controlling and punitive. The thoughtful teacher is able to take a breath, figure out what needs to happen, and then act on those thoughts. Maybe the answer is changing a troublemaker's seat, or sending a student to the office, or redirecting rambunctious students with an interesting question.

The Family Rules

All families have a set of rules, rules that represent their beliefs about how its members should behave and interact. The rules define the behavior expected in the car, what behavior can be tolerated and to what degree. Rules may be spoken aloud or left unspoken.

Rules That Promote Individuality

Families that encourage authenticity focus on the children and have rules that promote individual development, such as:

- People can be heard.
- If you have a complaint, someone is going to listen to you.
- People are supportive.
- People are advocated for.
- People are tolerant of each other's bad moods and fussiness.

In Lisa and Derrick's car, for example, it is expected that everyone will express their thoughts and feelings, and that they will listen to, support and advocate for each other. Charlie got to vent his frustration by stomping and yelling that he hates math—although, if he was expressing himself in a way that hurt others, that would not have been acceptable. Lisa and Derrick work hard to advocate for him, listen to him, and support him. It's okay if Lisa says she's angry at Mrs. Turner, if Derrick's patience gets maxed out from doing math homework, if Charlie is upset, or if Lionel is displeased with the choice of ice cream.

The rule is: Everyone is entitled to feel their feelings; we don't have to like it, and we can tolerate it.

The rules of the car also include boundaries around how each person treats the others. So, in a healthy car, you do what you need to do to be you, unless or until it infringes on another family member's needs. So, Lionel would be encouraged to express his feelings about the ice cream as long as he didn't retaliate against his brother.

In healthy cars, people work through conflict. They view conflict as a necessary part of growing and developing. It isn't pleasant or enjoyable, but it is inevitable, so it is a crucial skill for children to learn.

Rules That Don't Promote Individuality

Rules define behavior that is expected and tolerated in the family car, but that doesn't mean everyone likes, wants, or benefits from the behavior. It just means that it conforms to the rules of the car.

Some cars don't tolerate the expression of feelings. This is because it is uncomfortable for the parents. These parents don't understand that expressing feelings may benefit the children and may have rules like:

- Don't talk back.
- Don't question what mom or dad say.
- Put on a happy face even when you're unhappy.

In these cars, the adults unconsciously create rules that limit the expression of feelings. Rules like the ones above keep children from fully expressing themselves in order to keep the adults emotionally comfortable.

Conflict, particularly, can make certain parents uncomfortable, so some families tend to ignore it. In other cases, an authority figure has to win every conflict: "That's what I said!" or "This is the answer."

In one car, the father, Bill, suffers from untreated mental health issues. On some days, he's energetic and enthusiastic about life. He has great plans for the future that include making lots of money. On one such day, he takes his wife, Jeanne, and their two daughters, Dina and Rose, out to a fancy dinner. He's in a great mood, flirting with the waitress and ordering drinks and lots of desserts. He tells them they're going to go on a big vacation.

A few days later, Bill is lying in bed and can't get up. "You and the kids are all I have," he says hopelessly to Jeanne, holding her hand. "I've got nothing. I'm a failure. I'd be better off dead." Jeanne takes the kids to the movies to get them away from him and so she can relax. When they get home, she sends the kids to play in the backyard so she can check his mood before they go in.

The rule in their car is: We don't do anything that will upset Bill. Also: Nobody knows, on any given day, what will upset Bill.

One day, Dina leaves a toy on the floor and Jeanne asks her to pick it up. Bill yells at Jeanne that she's trying to get Dina to do her job. Another day, Dina leaves a toy out and Bill yells at her for leaving it out. Another day, he plays a game with the girls, leaves it out on the floor, and doesn't care that it's there.

Jeanne never gives him a reality check when he's flying high, and she keeps the kids away from him when he's low. This is a completely adult-centric car that is focused not on the growth of the children, but on the needs of the parents.

The rules don't work well to support the individual growth of each family member in a family like this, but by following them (or trying to), they manage to get from one day to the next together.

Breaking the Rules

When everyone follows the rules, the family car can continue down the road of life, from one day to the next. When the rules are challenged or broken, the car breaks down or has to change its rules in order to keep going.

We had two main rules in my family. The first was: Little girls are to be seen (looking nice and pretty) and not heard. That was the spoken rule. The unspoken rule was: Nobody is allowed to do anything that will upset mother. I followed those rules pretty well throughout my childhood. I tried to be independent and take care of myself and to be a good girl—not needy and not drawing attention to myself.

But when I was a senior in high school, very much against the rules of my car, I wrote a letter to the board of education about a teacher whose behavior felt unfair to me. It was so unusual for me to think that I had a voice and that I deserved to speak my truth. But according to my car's rules, I still wanted my mother's approval, so I asked her to read it. She berated me for speaking up and saying what I thought, saying that I could get someone in trouble and that I couldn't send it. I was challenging the rule of being voiceless in our car, and the result was that my mother did not talk to me for six weeks. Her silence was her attempt to restore the car to its normal homeostasis after I challenged the rule. And it worked—I never sent that letter.

Even if the rules don't suit everyone's well-being, they keep the car balanced, and each member works to keep that balance. When one person in the car, particularly a child, changes the way they behave, everyone else in the car will work to get that person back to their old behavior to maintain the balance. This is what keeps the car running and fulfills the basic human need to keep the car going.

For example, Jeanne's daughters, Dina and Rose, have conflict, as children do. Rose quietly needles Dina until she gets angry, and Dina gives her a shove. Dina is the "bully" and Rose is the "good girl." Dina doesn't want to be in trouble, so when Rose bugs her, she goes to Jeanne, who doesn't deal with the conflict until Dina loses her temper. She then scolds Dina and comforts Rose, reinforcing their roles.

These roles have both positive and negative aspects. As she gets older, Dina tends to see herself as powerful in her own life, and Rose tends to see herself as nice and likable. On the other hand, Dina thinks of herself as someone with a bad temper, and Rose often feels like a victim.

Where Do Family Rules Come From?

These rules come from the parents in the car, from their values and beliefs. In a two-parent family, parents basically combine the general themes of their lives, values, hopes, and expectations, and build their car's rules based on them. The rules are often not consciously thought out, discussed, or decided. In many families, the parents aren't even aware of the rules until children enter the picture, and each new child conforms to or challenges the rules.

Do you remember invisible ink books? They came with a special marker that revealed the answers to puzzles and questions. Children are like those markers, illuminating the family's invisible rules through their behavior and the parents' responses to their actions.

As a Family Develops, So Do the Rules

The primary purpose of rules is to keep the family from pushing the boundaries of what the car can emotionally tolerate.

It is natural for children to push these boundaries; this is how both children and parents learn and grow. Some of the most important lessons children learn are a result of making a mistake or breaking a rule. As children grow and develop, their needs should determine what the car provides, and the car should adapt in response to these challenges.

Each car contains people who are all going through the inevitable human processes of physical, emotional, and mental development. As a result, what the car expects and tolerates must evolve to accommodate these developmental changes.

As children grow, each developmental step they go through presents another challenge or change in behavior to which the car must adapt. The rules also adapt as new children come into the car and as other changes happen, such as a death or a grandparent or some other person moving in.

Rules change when a crying baby gives way to an exploring toddler, then to a child in school. They change when children become teenagers, when they move out (and when they move back in!), and so on.

When Charlie is in fourth grade, a certain amount of yelling and stomping is tolerated. But by the time he's a senior in high school, Lisa and Derrick may expect him to be better able to verbalize his feelings and participate in advocating for himself.

In a healthy car, children are expected to express themselves as they figure out who their authentic selves are. The message to them is: We, as a car, are going to tolerate this process, and the car is going to grow and adapt to your needs.

As children challenge the rules, sometimes the rules adapt to the challenges and sometimes the child has to conform to the rules.

The Rules of the Car Shape Us from Birth

When babies are born, they need love, comfort, and food. If these needs are consistently met, babies become secure in their attachment to their parents or caregivers. They learn that their needs matter, they are allowed to have needs, and the world will respond to their needs. If they're distressed, someone is there to help.

If a baby's needs are not met consistently enough (how often is enough depends on the child's DNA), they learn not to expect that someone will be there consistently enough for them when they are distressed.

This sense of attachment is solidified in our first year of life, and we base our expectations of other people on this understanding for the rest of our lives.

Every car has different rules about how much attention children should get and how to handle their distress. For example:

- Jerry is a parent who needs to be in control. PJ is a colicky baby who cries a lot, and it drives Jerry crazy. He believes that PJ will learn not to cry if his mother gives him less attention, and he strongly discourages Elena from going to PJ when he cries.
- Ebony and Josh have always attended to their babies

immediately, but once the babies start crawling and walking, it drives Ebony crazy trying to keep them out of the dog food and off of the kitchen table. To cope, the parents have the kids spend plenty of time in the pack 'n play.

- Elise just loved cuddling her babies, and she and her wife Martina had endless patience for chasing their son Mateo when he was a toddler. But the minute Mateo started saying no, around age three, they both felt he was misbehaving and needed a timeout whenever he challenged them.

In the first case, since PJ is left to cry too often, he does not trust that his mother will come to him and does not feel a secure attachment to either of his parents. He tends to cling to his mother as a small child and grows up to be intensely insecure in his relationships.

A secure attachment is also permanent, but it doesn't stop children from developing a whole cadre of negative behaviors to get attention. Because they need more attention and physical activity than they get, Ebony and Josh's kids chuck their toys out of the playpen all day—and, because Mateo's early expressions of independence were met with disapproval, he becomes rebellious and is in constant conflict with his moms as a teen.

Personality and Roles

Every human being has an innate temperament. Self-help books that aim to turn a dreamy, creative person into a checklist-driven "i" dotter and "t" crosser are promising something they cannot deliver. As babies begin to interact with the world around them, we see the temperament reveal itself.

They also instinctively find their own place in the family, expressing themselves and making sure they are noticed and loved as a unique individual. Children with older siblings will always try to be someone different than their older siblings; they are intentionally different because they want to be special and unique.

Our innate personalities are made up of different tendencies in different amounts, such as:

- Insightfulness, originality, curiosity, and openness to different thoughts, behaviors, feelings, and beliefs
- Tact, kindness, loyalty, compassion, and cooperativeness
- Carefulness, diligence, consistency, discipline, reliability, and ambition
- Being outgoing, assertiveness, warmth, and confidence
- Anxiety, instability, insecurity, fearfulness, and pessimism

These natural traits are neither negative nor positive, but how they are labeled in the car may be experienced as good or bad.

Behaviors deemed "good" get a positive response and behaviors deemed "bad" get a negative response. These repeated responses begin to solidify a child's role in the car and their label in the family.

For example, Dalia is called "the little firecracker" in her car. As a toddler, she was already climbing trees and bossing her older siblings around. She is seen as courageous and adventurous. She channels her abundant physical energy and natural assertiveness into sports, where she excels as a player, becomes team captain, and gets a college scholarship.

Lindy is also an energetic, physical little girl who is naturally gregarious and assertive—but in her car, these traits and behavior are seen as out of control, unladylike, not submissive enough to her parents, and too cocky—her parents call her "the troublemaker." Without a positive, car-approved outlet for her natural energy, she starts experimenting with drugs, being rude to her parents, and getting into trouble at school.

Roles and Labels

When Charlie was five, Derrick and Lisa took the family in a horse-drawn carriage. Charlie was mesmerized by the horses and couldn't talk about anything else for weeks, asking questions and demanding to watch videos of horses over and over. His parents were delighted and made sure to support his interest, taking him to a petting zoo and letting him stop to talk to mounted police in the park.

This was an expression of Lisa and Derrick's family rule about supporting their children's authentic selves, and as a result, Charlie learned that showing interest in something he enjoyed would please his parents and create opportunities to explore this interest. He also became known as the animal lover in the family. Whenever they met someone with a dog, his parents would call him over: "Charlie! Come see this beautiful dog." Lionel had a quick sense of humor and loved to make his family laugh all the time.

So, quite naturally, when Derrick was scrolling social media and found something funny, he was most likely to share it with Lionel; if he found a video of a baby elephant taking a bath, he called Charlie. Lionel became "the funny one" and Charlie became "the animal lover."

As PJ grew up, he learned that crying irritated his father and that keeping his emotions to himself made his father easier to get along with. He became quiet and withdrawn, spending more and more time alone in his room as he got older, and generally choosing not to share his feelings with anyone. "Oh, don't mind PJ," his parents would say at social gatherings, "He's the quiet one."

Reinforcement is a powerful tool that shapes our behavior and our roles in our families. This happens when behavior is reinforced in a positive way or a negative way. Reinforcement is any response to a behavior that increases the likelihood of it being repeated. This can be a positive or a negative response. Whether positively or negatively, we repeat behaviors that get reinforced.

In her family, Dina got a negative response from her parents from hitting Rose. Every time Jeanne warned Dina not to hit her sister, she saw herself more and more as the kid who was likely to hit. The negative response still served as a reward because it reinforced her negative identity. Similarly, a positive response reinforces a child's positive identity; either way, the child feels seen and acknowledged.

Half of how children learn who to be comes from their parents saying "no," and the other half comes from them saying "yes."

When Charlie shows an interest in animals, he gets opportunities to do things he loves; likewise, Lionel can always get a laugh from his family. On the other hand, when PJ is quiet, his father doesn't get annoyed with him. Charlie expresses interest, Lionel cracks jokes, PJ withdraws, and Dina smacks her sister. All of these actions reveal the roles in the car.

No matter the specifics of the family situation, repeated interactions reinforce certain behaviors, which children repeat until their roles in the car are defined.

Taking the Role Out of the Car

We all have a role and a label in our family car. And we absorb those roles and carry them out of our cars and into our adult lives, often without really realizing it.

If someone's role in the car is the black sheep, they may go out into the world expecting to be regarded as a black sheep and will probably act in ways that are counter to the culture or rules of any group they have contact with. They may seek out groups that they don't fit into, acting out their role over and over, or they may search until they find their "tribe," a group they fit in with, and adhere to that group with great loyalty and passion.

Instead of conforming to the role of nice quiet young lady, I went against my family's rules and became a social worker, a teacher, and a speaker—all ways in which I could be seen and heard.

As a parent, I decided that nobody in my family was going to feel like they weren't heard. My intended rule was that everyone would get the attention they needed. The actual rule was that everyone got the attention I thought they needed. In reality, my children are the determiners of what they need. So, every member of a family is likely to have slightly different perceptions of the rules. Each of my children certainly have their own views as to whether or not they got the attention they needed.

The challenge for us as adults is to examine our family's rules and our roles in our families, think about any "negative" ones we've carried into adulthood and ask ourselves, "Is it actually 'bad' or was it just considered bad in my family?" We can also look at rules and roles that may have been considered positive in our families but don't serve us well in our adult lives.

Following the rule of not crying and being "the quiet one" worked for PJ in his home growing up, but as an adult, he struggled with interactions and relationships, often withdrawing from people who liked and cared about him and were happy to let him be himself and feel his feelings.

Understanding what we took from our family car can help us understand how we interact with people and why. And it can help us make more thoughtful choices that serve us well in our adult lives.

Let's take a look at the rules in your family.

Ask Yourself

1. When something was troubling you in your family car, what did you do?
2. Did you feel there was someone you could go to when you were struggling?
3. Was your car a place where people could say what they needed to?
4. Did you feel like you could tell your parents when you were unhappy with them?
5. Did you feel like your family had each other's backs? Was empathy a value in your car?
6. What did you feel was expected of you in your car?
7. What was expected of the other members in the car? Were they different based on gender, birth order, abilities, etc.?
8. How do those rules affect your life and relationships today?
9. If you created a car as an adult, thinking back to

questions 1-7, what are the expectations and rules in
your car?

Notes

4
Types of Cars

Now that you understand rules and individual roles in the car, let's take a look at the four basic types of cars.

These types are defined by who is in the driver's seat and how the parents act in their relationships with each other and the children.

The point of understanding the types is to see how they affect how the children:

- Think about themselves
- See and experience other people
- Learn to relate to other people

Often, as parents, we don't realize how the rules of our car affect our children. When we understand these dynamics, we can choose to make changes. As you read these descriptions, you may think about what could be different in your family, how those changes could be helpful, and what it might take to make changes.

1. The Disconnected Car

Who's in the Driver's Seat?

In a disconnected car, no one is ever really in control. There's no one person the other people in this car can rely on to help them deal with life and move forward. While the parents may be very functional in their own endeavors, they are not engaged as parents.

A Snapshot of the Disconnected Car

Cherise and Cassidy are sisters sitting at their kitchen table. The back door opens, and the girls exchange a look. Their mother Denise comes in, pulling off her coat.

"I thought you were going to be home for dinner," says Cassidy. At 15, Cassidy is becoming a pretty good cook out of necessity. She has just finished making the quiche and salad she's sharing with her 12-year-old sister.

"We got behind at the office. You know how that goes. I just got done with my last patient."

"We waited, but we got hungry," says Cassidy. "You said you were coming home."

"That's fine," says her mother, hanging her coat up by the door and picking up the mail, "I had Jenna get me a sandwich at the office."

Cherise shakes her head and rolls her eyes. Cassidy returns the look.

"Oh yeah," says Cassidy, "Horizons called. There was a message on the landline. You were supposed to set up a family session with Jack and Dr. Moore. We're all supposed to go."

"Well, Daddy's in Guatemala building that hospital. He's not going to be back until next month."

"Will you at least call them?"

"What? Oh, sure," says Denise, pulling a bottle of wine out of the fridge and pouring a glass. Her general attitude toward her18-year-old son Jack's opioid addiction is that it's like some mysterious force that is completely beyond her control. So as long as he's in rehab it's easy for her to pretend it's not happening.

"And I need you to sign the paper for driver's ed. I signed up, but they won't let me drive without a parent's signature."

"Okay. Leave it here."

"Can you do it now? I need it tomorrow, remember?"

Denise looks up. "I'll do it. Just leave it here."

Cassidy stares at her, frustrated and annoyed.

What do they want out of me? Denise wonders. *I do everything I can for them.*

Cassidy takes a breath and looks at her another moment, about to say something, but changes her mind and turns to her sister.

"Cher, it's time for that math. Let's go. In the den."

Her sister picks up her backpack and follows her out of the room. Denise stays in the kitchen, drinking her wine.

What Kids Learn in the Disconnected Car

The key beliefs Cassidy and Cherise have developed are: "No one is there for me. I don't matter. I'm not important. If I'm going to make it in this world, I'm going to have to do it myself."

Kids from disconnected cars don't feel cared about. They feel like their parents are not investing in them, so they often don't understand that they deserve to be cared for, that as adults, their parents could take care of them, assist them, put them first, and that their needs matter.

Denise and her husband do not provide leadership, structure, or routine for Cassidy and Cherise. Life is all about putting out fires, like making dinner, signing a driver's ed permission form, or making a family therapy appointment. There is no continuity and no goal-driven behavior in their car.

Neither of these parents is going to say, "Gee, there are always papers we need to sign that are turned in late, which is frustrating and stressful for the kids; we need a place to put things the kids need signed. Okay, if they leave something right here, I'll see it and sign it." And they're not aware of their kids' needs or feelings about these things.

These kids grow and develop without a role model who shows them how to tackle a task or process. They don't learn that if something isn't working, they can look at it, think about how to do it differently, and learn and grow from that process. Their experience is, "Life is just going to come at me. I'm going to swipe at it however I can and just try to move to the next day."

No one tells these kids that they are entitled to try, fail, learn, and succeed. No one says, "Go ahead—you can do this! I'll help you." What they do feel entitled to do is sneak or cheat or do things that are against the law because it's the only way they can feel they are valuable, or that they have something to offer.

The disconnected car is the worst functioning family because it fails to teach children that they can affect the outcome of a situation. These kids tend to grow up not knowing, understanding, or believing that they can set goals, figure out steps to meet them, and take those steps. Life feels scary: "I don't know what's going to happen to me. If something does happen to me, I don't know who will be there with me and help me through it." It can feel like they're banging through life blindly.

Characteristics

- No one dependably in driver seat
- No dependable leadership
- Driven by parental needs rather than children's needs
- No dependable structure with predictable approval or consequences for behaviors
- Feelings are ignored

- No knowledge of each unique child
- Family doesn't learn and grow from experiences
- Tend not to promote teamwork among the children
- No follow through
- Putting out fires daily before moving on to the next day

2. The Controlled Car

Who's in Control

Some cars have a dictator, a person who feels the need to control the minds, behaviors, and feelings of every person in the car because they think they know what's best for everyone, or is so insecure that they must control their environment. Everyone in the car goes along with what the dictator requires of them. The dictator has absolute power and will dictate more harshly to anyone who threatens it. The dictator controls through fear. People in the car don't like the consequences of not doing what the dictator wants.

Dictators are unable to take influence or consider others' opinions. They don't consider the individual needs of the family members and have difficulty seeing other people's points of view.

An extreme example of a dictator controlling a car is a family where there is domestic abuse or domestic violence. These are controlled cars where one person is in control and everyone's job is to comply and do whatever that person wants because they are afraid not to. In other controlled families, the fear may not be physical but more about not wanting to be a disappointment, or about not wanting to stir the pot because it will change the general mood in the family.

A Snapshot of the Controlled Car

Marla is standing in the kitchen, an oven mitt on one hand and a wooden spoon in the other. She has managed to get her three daughters, six-year-old Kayla, four-year-old Chance, and three-year-old Rennie to stop moving for the first time all day, and they're coloring at the table while she makes dinner. She hears the door to the garage slam in a particularly angry way. Her body tenses and she wonders tiredly: *Now what?*

Her husband Jerry is home from work. He walks in holding up a pamphlet and when Marla recognizes it, she thinks: *Oh shoot.*

He stops at the table and kisses each of the girls on the head, but he's glaring at Marla over their heads. Then he walks over and stands close to her by the stove.

"What the hell?" he asks, his voice low. He holds up the pamphlet. "And who leaves their purse in the car? Are you going behind my back?" He waves the pamphlet at her again.

"No, I mean…I just had my hands full coming in the house."

He cocks his head, looking angry and betrayed, a look that usually means a scene is coming. It's the end of a long day and she was hoping to get through dinner, bath time, and bedtime with time left to be able to sit down and fold some laundry in front of the TV. *Please, God*, she thinks, *not now.*

"I just saw the doctor today for a checkup. She just thought— she suggested, you know, since…" Her voice trails off.

"Your doctor doesn't have the slightest idea what's best for this family," says Jerry.

"No, she wasn't suggesting—"

"Tubal ligation?" he says. "No way. We agreed. This is what we wanted for our kids. A big happy family. A mom at home. A house full of noise and kids to play with. That's the best way to raise kids. We had a deal. Remember?"

Jerry grew up an only child. His mother struggled with depression and his father travelled. Jerry was alone a lot as a kid, and when he and Marla got married, they agreed on a big family. With three girls under six and a baby on the way, Marla feels like the family is big enough, especially since Jerry has very "old-fashioned" ideas about who should make a living and who should do 100 percent of the childcare and housekeeping.

"Yes, of course, but look at the girls," says Marla, her voice a little too bright. "They have each other and they're going to have a little brother soon. That's a pretty big family these days!"

44

"No," says Jerry, a little loudly. The girls look up. "We had a deal and I'm more than holding up my end. I worked my butt off building this business so you could stay home, and this is what I get?"

He waves the pamphlet again. "This is just complete disrespect," he says, shaking his head. "Complete disrespect."

Marla glances at the oven timer. "I have to check that," she says, ducking her face as she looks at the lasagna so Jerry won't see the tears welling up in her eyes. She's tired all the time and was thinking that after their new baby was old enough, she could go back to nursing part-time and use the money for daycare a few days a week. It feels like she hasn't been away from her children since Kayla was born and she needs a break. Jerry doesn't "babysit," so she rarely sees friends, and soon she's going to be nursing 'round the clock again because Jerry doesn't believe in formula. But she also feels guilty. *He's right*, she thinks. *We had a deal. Of course he's mad.*

"Daddy," calls Kayla, looking a little anxious. "Come look at my picture. I drew you a picture!"

Jerry gives Marla a look and walks over the table. She mouths "I'm sorry" and gives him a weak, apologetic smile.

"Hey baby. Let's see. Oh wow, that's just great," he says to Kayla, relaxing slightly.

Marla exhales, relieved this hasn't turned into yelling, the kids crying, dinner ruined as it so easily could have. But she is concerned that Kayla has started regularly interrupting these exchanges. *Is she intentionally trying to diffuse the conflict?* wonders Marla, glancing at her daughter.

Living in the Controlled Car

Jerry is in control. He is not concerned about Marla's feelings or autonomy or about the atmosphere he is creating for the children. Marla and the children try very hard to behave in ways that will not make him angry, and fear of his response governs almost every decision and action in their family.

In a controlled car, one parent often uses anger to manipulate and control and the other does what they think they "should" in order to avoid the anger. The controller feels they need to ensure everyone does what they're supposed to do so they get the best outcome, and the other parent thinks, consciously or unconsciously, *I just need to do what they tell me I should. I just need to try harder. I'm not doing it well enough.*

The anger is frightening to the kids in the controlled car, and they focus on finding ways to feel safe. Before adolescence, they don't resist and tend to go along with the family rules, because the other parent has shown them that's what you do. For example, Kayla has started trying to mollify Jerry when he's upset because that's what Marla does. The rule is: We don't upset daddy.

The unspoken rule in many controlled cars is that no one can talk about the family's controlling behaviors or fears outside of the family. In dangerous controlled families, the kids' reality is often denied by both the controlling parent and the parent who complies or enables.

Because these cars are driven by the parents' needs, the kids often feel like they don't matter, and it becomes a deep identity for them. They feel like they are not "enough," which leads to feeling unlovable and often angry.

When the kids in the controlled car become adolescents and start being able to make choices and decisions, they often look for ways to numb the pain of the control and fear and secrets. It's common for them to start drinking or doing drugs. Adolescent girls in these families often become very promiscuous because they're looking for the love and acceptance they didn't receive at home. Adolescent boys start exhibiting the same controlling behaviors— especially toward women if they grew up in a heterosexual family.

Quiet vs. Noisy Control

Some controlled cars are noisy, yelling cars, where these tactics are used to control everyone. Some controlled cars are quietly controlled cars where the rule is that everyone keeps their feelings to themselves.

In many controlled cars, the fear, whether of physical violence or emotional damage, is never spoken of, discussed, or validated for the children who live in it. As a result, the kids grow up in fear. They also can't talk about it with anyone, which makes things very difficult for them.

People from a controlled car tend to go in two directions as adults.

Some people who are in a controlled car rebel, and their life is just about being anything but how their car wanted them to be. When they finally have the freedom to be whoever they want, they know they don't want to be how they were raised to be. This is not necessarily bad, just different. In my case, I became a teacher and a speaker, which went against the rules of little girls being seen and not heard in my family's car, but in a good way.

Other people in a controlled car create their own controlled cars because they think that is how you move forward. These are parents that are highly critical of their children: "Sit up straight. Eat right. You can't have dessert before you have this." That type of control and order is actually anxiety reducing for a lot of parents who grew up the same way, so they try to create the same environment for themselves.

Characteristics

- Dictator in the driver's seat
- Controlled by fear
- Tries to control the thoughts and behaviors of everyone in the car because "they know best"
- Can quietly control with fear or can be a noisy controlled car with yelling
- Control is often an unspoken, even silent, private experience that creates secrets for kids
- Things are black or white, good or bad
- No room for authenticity
- No feelings allowed other than dictator's anger
- No challenges to the homeostasis allowed

- Control is rigid and based on the needs of the dictator, not the children or circumstances

3. The Perfect Car

Who's In Control

The perfect car is controlled by an idea: the car's idea of what everyone in the car "should" do and be.

In the perfect car, love and attention are meted out in response to being and behaving in accordance with the rules. Everyone in the car tries to do and be what they "should," because in the perfect car, that's how you get love and attention.

The perfect car basically plays on people's guilt and perfectionism, driving them to look how they should, get the grades they should, have the job they should, behave the way they should, and so on.

A Snapshot of the Perfect Car

It's 6:30 am on the day after Halloween and seven-year-old Haley is sitting at the breakfast table with Alexis, looking at the pictures of her in her cheerleader costume.

"Oh my god," says Alexis, "you look just perfect, even better than last year—you were still a little pudgy then."

Haley smiles at her mother and turns her attention to her fruit bowl and dry toast. Scotty and Trip come down the stairs, followed by their father, Dan.

"How would you like your eggs?" Alexis asks them.

Trip says "Sunny-side up" at the same time Dan says "Scrambled," and they both laugh.

"Honey, I'll eat sunny-side up if it's easier, but I am going to have to leave for the airport soon." He checks his watch. "I'm presenting at the National Hospital meeting at 3:00, but I'm coming home tomorrow—I have a Chamber of Commerce meeting."

"Scotty, sunny-side up, okay?"

"Can I have toast and peanut butter?"

"Oh. Sure." Alexis has been up since 5 am. She's gotten in her workout, a shower, and made lunches before everyone came down for breakfast. She is wearing a matching slacks and sweater set, hair, make-up, and nails all done.

"You look great, by the way, honey," says Dan. Alexis smiles at him, glances at the eggs in the pan, and then goes to the refrigerator to check the family calendar.

"Okay, Trip—game tonight, right?"

"Yep. Planning to hunt some WB crocodile!" Trip says, miming stalking the opponent's mascot.

"Okay, well I have a client at four, but I will be there for the PTA tailgate. I made a huge tray of mac and cheese and a batch of chocolate chip cookies," says Alexis, serving the eggs and pulling toast out of the toaster. "Scotty, honey, maybe you'll put down the video game long enough to watch your brother play?"

Ten-year-old Scotty looks at his shoes. "Yeah, sure."

"And Trip, you need a check for your choir gown," says Alexis, handing Trip an envelope.

"Football and choir—in middle school! Perfect, buddy, you are so on track to get into the old alma mater," says Dan. "How fun would it be to go to football games and see Trip playing and Haley cheering?"

"So fun," says Scotty, focusing on his toast.

"Oh geez," says Dan looking at his watch, "Gotta go." He grabs his carry-on bag and his briefcase, kisses Alexis, and heads out the door. "See you guys tomorrow!"

Life in the Perfect Car

In the perfect car, everyone in the car knows that they need to look a certain way, act a certain way, dress a certain way, and take a certain route in their life. For example, in Alexis and Dan's car, the kids need to go to school, get specific grades, and participate in particular extracurricular activities so they can get into Alexis and Dan's alma mater. Also, they should be slim and well-dressed. There's no questioning. The perfect car is the car of "shoulds."

That perfect car's values come from many different places. They come from:

- Geographical location
- People who live around us on our street
- People who go to school with us
- The larger society that tells us through the media what's good and what's not good
- Religion, ethnicity, or national origin

Every family follows a set of social norms. In the perfect family, however, members believe they are only worthwhile and deserving of love if they adhere to those norms.

For example, Dan wants to be a good, perfect father. In his "perfect" family, a good father "should" go to work during the week and come home and spend time with the kids on the weekend. One weekend, he is invited to go fishing with friends and finds himself in a dilemma: "I want to be a good father, but if I go fishing, am I not a good enough father?" It leaves him feeling guilty and resentful.

The "should" is an absolute. In some families, a father can be good and have a fishing weekend—but in the perfect family, people often do what they "should" instead of what they want. Children from perfect cars often don't know what they want, even as adults.

The family members, particularly the children, believe love is obtained by conforming to a certain standard rather than believing that they are inherently good, worthwhile, and deserving of love. They have to do or be something in order to deserve love.

Characteristics

- Control comes from each person looking for love and approval
- Children act how they think they should to get love and affection

- The car of "shoulds"
- Based on the family's culture, socio-economic status, gender roles, and so on
- List of preexisting shoulds for a mother, father, daughter, and son
- Authentic feelings are not allowed
- "Stiff upper lip" houses
- Looking good is important
- Perfectionist children
- All members must look a certain way, act a certain way, follow a certain path in their life
- Oppressive atmosphere due to the suppression of authenticity
- Confusion over who each person really is

4. The Real Car

Who's in Control

In the real car, there is a firm but flexible structure that provides a predictable routine. A firm structure is important because children in the car need to know everyone must follow some rules in life, and they need to learn how to follow rules. But the strength of the real car is that the firm structure is flexible. The structure flexes according to the needs of each person.

A Snapshot of a Real Car

Dinner is over and Janelle looks meaningfully at her children.

Tamara quickly says, "It's not my turn."

"Oh yes, it is," says Keith. "Nice try, though."

Tamara, caught, laughs and goes to the sink to wash the dishes. Keith stays at the table with his mom. He looks at the fourth chair for a moment. Although they stopped setting a place about two years after Harley died, they still think of it as "Dad's chair."

"You okay?" asks his mother.

A tear spills over and rolls down Keith's cheek. Janelle reaches behind her to get a box of tissues off the side table and hands it to him.

"Some days I really miss him, you know?"

"Yeah, I sure do," says Janelle.

"I think it's going to go away, or I think I'm better, and then one day, I just think about him and want to cry all day."

"I know. Did something happen today?"

"No. Well, yeah. Not so much something happened, but I was driving by that place Dad got the car stuck in a ditch when we were driving around looking at Christmas lights that time."

"Yeah, some days that one makes me laugh and some days it makes me cry and sometimes both."

"Yeah, exactly," says Keith.

Tamara comes back to the table. She looks at the chair too.

Janelle looks at her. Tamara was never quite the cheerful creature her brother is, but that blank sad look wasn't her default expression before Harley's death, and it hurts Janelle's heart. She puts her hand over Tamara's, but Tam pulls it away.

"Hey, why don't we have a game night?" Janelle asks. "Friday? You could invite your friends over and I'll order pizza. What do you think?"

"I don't really feel like hanging out with people right now," says Tam. "I'm a little stressed out about mid-terms and people just take too much energy."

"Yeah?"

"Yeah, they all seem either happy or their problems seem stupid. Either way, it kind of feels like they don't know how good they have it."

"Yes, well..."

The kids finish the well-worn family joke, chanting, "This sucks, plain and simple."

Keith smiles. Even Tamara manages something that's more than a grimace.

"Yeah, it does," says Janelle.

"I'm going to go to bed," says Tamara. It's early, but Janelle knows she just needs to be alone.

"Okay honey. Sweet dreams. And if you change your mind, the pizza offer is open."

"Okay, thanks, but I don't think so."

Keith and Janelle sit there quietly for a moment. The doorbell rings.

"Oh, hey, I forgot. Xander's here to study for history."

"Okay honey. I've got some briefs to work on. You guys can have the kitchen. I'll be in my office."

How the Real Car Functions

In the real car, there is no single truth. Everybody knows that each member has a lot of different emotions, and the real car is open to hearing them, dealing with them, and making those emotions a part of the fiber of the car. As a result:

- There's nothing that can't be said or spoken about.
- There are no secrets that need to be kept.
- Everyone has the option to be open with each individual, or within various dyads or triads in the family.
- The core belief is: "We can say what we need to in this car and the car can tolerate it."

Janelle, Keith, and Tamara all have feelings about Harley's death. They all express them and do what they need to do for themselves. It's different for each of them, and each of them makes room for what the others feel and need to do.

A real family might be rowdy, loud, or noisy. People might be frustrated. Somebody might be mad at another family member. It might look all kinds of different ways. It's often messy.

It isn't a bunch of people sitting and not expressing themselves in order for the car to be quiet or not quiet. It's about the car being a place where everyone feels that they can express what they need to express in order to be able to do what they want to do in their life.

Being able to say what you need to and about the other person, your relationship, and the difficulties in your life is what keeps people close, and that's what happens in the real car.

The goal of the car is ultimately to launch everyone. So, people in real families are close to each other, they know each other, they know their emotions, they trust each other, and they have each other's backs. People raised in a real car often leave their car and create other real cars because they're used to having people to process life with in an honest way, people who have their back, who are nonjudgmental, who respect what they want, and who want the best for them.

Characteristics

- Firm but flexible leadership, often alternating between parents with agreed upon values
- Firm but flexible structure, changing to meet the needs of a growing family
- The strengths and challenges of each member are acknowledged and tended to
- Acceptance and tolerance are key within the structure of the family
- Emotions are expected and encouraged, heard and processed
- Life is processed and learned from
- Risk is encouraged and failure is expected and soothed
- Real cars are messy

The Disconnected Car	The Controlled Car
<ul><li>No one dependably in driver seat</li><li>No dependable leadership</li><li>Driven by parental needs rather than children's needs</li><li>No dependable structure with predictable approval or consequences for behaviors</li><li>Feelings are ignored</li><li>No knowledge of each unique child</li><li>Family doesn't learn and grow from experiences</li><li>Tend not to promote teamwork among the children</li><li>No follow through</li><li>Family puts out fires daily before moving on to the next day</li></ul>	<ul><li>Dictator in the driver's seat</li><li>Controlled by fear</li><li>Tries to control the thoughts and behaviors of everyone in the car because "they know best"</li><li>Can quietly control with fear or can be a noisy controlled car with yelling</li><li>Control is often an unspoken, even silent, private experience that creates secrets for kids</li><li>Things are black or white, good or bad</li><li>No room for authenticity</li><li>No feelings allowed other than dictator's anger</li><li>No challenges to the homeostasis allowed</li><li>Control is rigid and based on the needs of the dictator, not the children or circumstances</li></ul>
The Perfect Car	The Real Car
<ul><li>Control comes from each person looking for love and approval</li><li>Children act how they think they should to get love and affection</li><li>The car of "shoulds"</li><li>Based on the family's culture, socio-economic status. gender roles, and so on</li><li>Preexisting "shoulds" for a mother, father, daughter, and son</li><li>Authentic feelings are not allowed</li><li>"Stiff upper lip" houses</li><li>Looking good is important</li><li>Perfectionist children</li><li>All members must look a certain way, act a certain way, follow a certain path in their life</li><li>Oppressive atmosphere due to the suppression of authenticity</li><li>Confusion over who each person really is</li></ul>	<ul><li>Firm but flexible leadership, often alternating between parents with agreed upon values</li><li>Firm but flexible structure, changing to meet the needs of a growing family</li><li>The strengths and challenges of each member are acknowledged and tended to</li><li>Acceptance and tolerance are key within the structure of the family</li><li>Emotions are expected and encouraged, heard and processed</li><li>Life is processed and learned from</li><li>Risk is encouraged and failure is expected and soothed</li><li>Real cars are messy</li></ul>

Ask Yourself

1. Which of these cars feels most like the car(s) you grew up in (many people grow up in families that are a combination or that change over time)?
2. Looking at the list of characteristics above, which ones characterized your family?
3. Sometimes coming to this understanding about the family we grew up in brings up a lot of emotions. What does this bring up for you?

Notes

_____

_____

_____

_____

_____

_____

_____

_____

_____

_____

_____

_____

_____

_____

_____

_____

_____

_____

_____

_____

_____

_____

5
Life Happens, Cars Change

As you read about different kinds of families, you may have compared the car you grew up in to the car you created as an adult, and it may feel like comparing apples and oranges. That's because you are. Families have changed.

To some extent, prior to the mid-'60s, we all grew up in "perfect" cars. When men came back from WWII and the baby boom began, every family in every culture in our country tried to achieve the American dream, and that dream looked pretty much the same for everyone. You went to school, got married, bought a house, and had a family—and then you got to retire and watch your children do the same thing. Houses looked alike, people got similar jobs, women stayed home, and men went to work.

In that time, there was little attention paid to individual differences. Everybody was supposed to fit into a traditional perfect car.

But the mid-'60s also brought attention to human rights movements. Suddenly, as a society, we were talking about and working toward women's rights and civil rights. We recognized that women wanted the same rights as men. People of color's fight for equal rights entered the national spotlight, and President Lyndon B. Johnson pushed to legislate for increased individual rights for many different groups.

As an individual, you were suddenly allowed to look at yourself, no matter who you were and what your circumstances, and think: *I can be my full, authentic self and still deserve a place in society.*

The advent of birth control pills created a monumental change in women's lives and to the structure of the family. Prior to the pill, if women had sex, they had children. They didn't have a choice and they didn't have a voice. They stayed in their marriages. The pill changed the amount of power women had over their lives and in society, allowing for a range of choices that would reshape the culture and the family.

But it wasn't just women and minorities who felt the growing need for personal freedom. All individuals were feeling a greater need to figure out who they were and be that way.

This sense of personal freedom has created a disconnect between generations, with an older generation that sees conformity as the ideal and a younger generation that fervently believes in individuality.

Families are struggling because children born now know they have more freedom than their parents who were born prior to the '60s. Even if that is not true in their car, the culture around them is a giant kaleidoscope of infinite choices, and the message kids get today is that they are all equally acceptable.

As you examine your family, it's important to be aware that it's not the same family as your grandparents' family or your parents' family. How you were raised may have been really good for the time you lived in, but children of the future have very different needs. Families need to understand that to create cars where children can truly achieve their full potential.

Thoughts beginning "When I was a kid" just don't apply.

But the dynamics described in Chapter 4 do. For example, in previous generations, in a real car, although the expectation would have been that you did what you should, your feelings about it would be recognized and accepted. And in a disconnected, controlled, or perfect car, that was less true.

For example, if everyone went to the high school football game on Friday nights, the whole family would go. But in the real car, it would be okay that one sibling found football boring and hated sitting on cold bleachers while another couldn't get enough and would scream themselves silly cheering on the home team. In the disconnected, controlled, or perfect car, you would just go and keep your feelings to yourself.

Prior to this generational shift, people tended not to talk about aspects of their cars that were unique. If a girl in my class had two mommies, she would have kept it quiet—and if I found out about it, I certainly wouldn't have gone home and talked about it.

Today, a schoolchild could openly talk about a classmate with two mommies or a friend's baby sister who has a birth defect. Prior to this shift, a baby born with differing abilities was a tragic secret, something to hide. Now that baby is rightly seen and encouraged to see herself as a full human being with rights and an equal expectation to live a fulfilling, satisfying life.

Family structures have needed to change dramatically in response to society's changing view of the individual. Some of these changes have created dramatic shifts in individual families. Rising divorce rates are leading to more instances of single parent homes, children living in two homes, remarriages, blended families, and so forth.

How Do We Deal with a Changing Family?

If you live in a changing family, the seats in your car may shuffle. Your individual role in the family or families you are a part of may change, and it may feel like your identity related to that role is being challenged.

How do children navigate that? They wonder: *Am I still the oldest? What seat do I sit in? What is my identity?*

When a family changes, the dynamics that create and reinforce individual roles change too. Suddenly, there are different expectations. The car may even become a different kind of car. Kids lose their roles and identities when a family changes and are left trying to figure out who they are.

In an atmosphere where people are trying to figure out who they are to be true to themselves, our cars are changing more frequently than they ever have. It can leave people feeling like there's something wrong with them because they don't have a stable car like they think other people do.

Life is not static. Events happen to us and around us all the time, and some of them cause dramatic changes in our cars. In this chapter, we are going to talk about what happens when people enter or leave a car, and how different types of cars tend to deal with seismic shifts in the family.

The Empty Seat

When a family suffers the loss of a parent or child, there is an empty seat. Each type of family recognizes, responds to, and reorganizes around this empty seat in a different way.

Disconnected Family

Disconnected families tend not to openly acknowledge the loss or the family members' feelings about it. The parents don't comfort a child dealing with loss, invite the child to express their feelings, or help the child process the experience. The child is left to make sense of the loss and cope with their grief alone.

Controlled Family

In controlled families, the dictator choreographs everyone's responses to minimize genuine feelings. Because control is so often about avoiding negative emotions, the dictator in the controlled car will often say something like "We're not going to talk about it anymore," or "This isn't the time to bring it up." They may not even need to say it—the children can sense from the dictator's behavior or mood what they can and cannot talk about. The dictator doesn't want to feel painful emotions and they don't want anyone to make them feel them.

Perfect Family

In perfect families, everyone does what they "should" as determined by their family culture (which includes socio-economic status, ethnicity, race, gender, and so on). People pay very little attention to feelings and are often expected to "soldier up." In my practice, one client's mom died when she was 12 after years battling cancer. After she died, she was never mentioned in the family again, so as to not bring up a difficult subject. Another client lost a sister to cancer when they were both in elementary school, and the sister's place was still set at the table as long as the client lived at home (and probably after). Even with this, there was no talk of feelings or of processing the loss.

Real Families

Real families talk about things appropriately at the time of the loss, whenever something comes up and family members need and want to process and share their feelings, and at each new developmental stage of the children. The person who died is referred to forever: "It is so sad that Mom isn't here on this most special day." Conversations are meant to bring forth all of the internalized emotion with the view that it isn't good to hold on to it.

Divorce or Separation

Divorce rates are currently at their lowest point in 50 years, but we are also seeing far fewer marriages. Whether parents are married or not, when they separate, the car changes. A seat is left unfilled. Children may have to navigate two cars, possibly with different seats, roles, and rules in each one. Maybe in mom's car, they can get away with anything, but in dad's car, things are very strict.

Kids know what's going on in each car and they work hard to get what they can get, even if it means lying or pitting their parents against each other. It's particularly hard when the parents don't communicate, because children in these situations really need to be coparented. Some kids find their way through these challenges, but some find them very confusing.

They all have feelings about it, and very frequently, the parents stifle the children's feelings because of their own guilt, shame, and anger. These are common elements across all types of cars, but, as with all changes, they are processed differently in different types of cars.

Disconnected Car

In disconnected cars, children are not helped to process the event, and no one attempts to soothe their feelings. The parents think the kids will "get used to it" or that "they're resilient and they'll adjust." In these families, parents often blame each other for the divorce and share their reasons and grievances with the kids.

Controlled Car

In a controlled car, the controller may no longer be in charge of the car where the kids spend most of their time. The process of the new, non-controlled car finding its own style can be difficult and confusing for the kids, and in these situations, they often don't have a parent helping them through it. The controller frequently still controls both cars, in which case processing emotions would make the controller feel emotions they don't want to feel. As a result, doing so is discouraged. However the new car functions, these kids are often not helped to deal with the emotions they feel about the changes.

Perfect Car

In perfect cars, there may be much unexpressed shame and guilt, since divorce isn't usually something people in perfect cars believe they "should" do. The goals in these families are about looking good from the outside, so its members continue doing the other "shoulds," achieving in work and school, looking perfect, and so on. The kids are expected to just carry on and no one acknowledges or helps them process their feelings of loss, anger, and fear.

Real Car

In real cars, the parents tell their children about the divorce together. The parents don't assign blame for the divorce and the narrative is usually that the parents don't love each other anymore, but they both still and will always love the children. The parents' goal is to help the children work through their feelings, and their energy is directed at making the transition as easy as possible for the children rather than fulfilling their own needs.

The Newly Single Family

In the newly single family, there is suddenly an empty seat. It can be the seat of the parent who has left this car; later, if that absent parent's seat gets filled, it may then be vacated by the person who took it. Either way, the roles of other family members may change as a result of the vacancy. There may be a new driver or a new second in command. One child may hop into the seat vacated by the other parent or adult; relationships and alliances within the family may shift as roles and rules change and family members try to adjust to both the changes and their emotions about them.

Disconnected Family

In the disconnected family, this shift is acknowledged less because whoever is in the driver's seat in these families tends to be transitory. The emotional toll of the change is still there, however, and will get acted out or internalized as shame or guilt by the children.

The Controlled Family

If the controller moves out of the home, this family often becomes disconnected because no one in this car knows how to take control. In the controller's new car, things generally stay the same because the dynamic of the controller avoiding any emotion remains the defining influence in the family.

The Perfect Car

This is a crisis to the perfect homeostasis and the car must reorganize, which can take time. It can become a disconnected car, or it can morph into a more real car due to the realization that the family isn't perfect.

The Real Car

In the real car, the family talks about the changes with only one parent in the car. They generally stay a real family and always have room to talk about the changes.

Blending Families

Many kids who become part of a blended family have gone through a death or divorce and found homeostasis again in a single parent car, possibly with one of the children sitting in the passenger seat where a second parent used to be. That child gets a positive identity as an important helper in the family, and the parent has a buddy they can rely on. Then, once the parent finds a partner or remarries, that child gets displaced again.

When members of more than one family move in together, the seats, roles, rules, and even the type of car it is can all change—for example, the oldest may not be the oldest anymore. Each developmental stage has its own set of struggles with this situation. Teens may be more critical about their parents for causing the change, for example, whereas elementary school-aged children may try hard to be loyal to both parents.

Blending a family is an opportunity for both parents to really think about what they want for their children and how to achieve it by setting new rules. In the beginning, for at least two years, there should be a rule that the natural parent does the disciplining of their own child. The kids in these families are dealing with loss. It's a trauma, and it can't be glossed over. Blended families require tremendous communication between the parents. It has to be a purposeful, intentional experience for it to work, especially if there are any teenagers in the bunch. Second marriage divorce rates are so high because the blending is a huge crisis to the existing homeostasis of each family. But that same crisis also, almost always, provides an opportunity to move toward realness.

Regardless of their ages and the specifics of the process, children have a lot of feelings about these adjustments and are contending with a new dynamic around processing their emotions. Each type of car handles this differently.

Disconnected Car

In disconnected cars, children are expected to just go along with whatever is happening in the house. Their feelings are ignored. Teens at this stage often internalize or act out their feelings. This dynamic can be particularly challenging for children who are used to a real or controlled family.

Controlled Car

In controlled families, children do what they are told to do, which often leaves them little room for or interest in expressing feelings. Kids in these blended families often have animus toward each other, and life can become a competition to get the attention they need. Sometimes it is by being the bad one and sometimes by being the peacekeeper.

Perfect Car

In perfect families, everyone is expected to go along and continue to obey the "shoulds." There is often a great deal of competition in these families, too, as well as negative "acting in" behaviors like drug abuse or suicide attempts. The perfect child may continue on their quest for perfection, however that looks to them.

Real Car

The real family talks about hard adjustments and understand-able negative emotions during these changes. The real family is messy. Kids are unhappy and upset and the real family talks about it while still observing a firm structure to increase stability for the kids. This can be tricky with two different family structures, but the parents have a mutual commitment to it.

Ask Yourself

1. Did the family you grew up in or the family you created as an adult go through one (or more) of these changes? If so, which one(s)?
2. How did your role shift as a result of the change?
3. How did the roles of other family members change?
4. What were the rules of the car before the change? After?
5. How did you feel about the change?
6. How were feelings handled around the change in your family?

Notes

_____

_____

_____

_____

_____

_____

_____

_____

_____

_____

_____

_____

_____

_____

_____

_____

_____

_____

_____

_____

_____

_____

_____

_____

_____

6
Compassion for the Kid in the Car

If we were chatting face to face, I would ask you how you feel about what you've learned. Since we're not face to face, I would like to say that this kind of work brings up many feelings, and the reason I wrote this book was to try to help you to develop compassion for yourself for being the person in your seat in your car.

Sometimes this knowledge brings a sigh of relief or an "aha" moment and sometimes it makes us sad or brings up pain from the past. If it makes you sad, I'd like you to imagine yourself as a small child of six or younger. Try to imagine how those feelings felt then, for that small child. If you were the parent of that small child and you knew they were having those feelings, what might you say to that child to acknowledge and perhaps alleviate their pain?

My hope is that you might speak to yourself as an adult with that same compassionate voice. In addition to soothing those old hurts, another reason I wrote the book is that I hope people who find that compassionate voice bring it into their current cars.

Being part of a family is an intense experience, filled with moments of heightened emotion, and I would like for people to be able to use compassion in those instances rather than other ways of alleviating their emotions.

We can't have compassion for others unless we have it for ourselves. If we didn't develop it in our family car, then learning to do it becomes our task as adults.

My vision is for more compassionate cars that create a more compassionate world.

So, what does compassion mean here?

Think back to when you were small and learning to ride a bicycle and you fell and scraped your knee. There are many ways a parent could respond to that, but a compassionate parent's response starts with acknowledging that you fell and hurt yourself and that you're in distress. "Oh, you fell—that must have scared you." But when parents can't access compassion for their child, they may respond in a negative fashion, trying to overlook the injury or invalidating it, saying, "You're okay—just get back up." They may get angry: "You didn't do what I told you to do!"

We all fall in life, and it's not because we were wrong or bad or not listening. We just fall. It's impossible to live life and not fall. Life is hard and full of falls for both children and adults, and if we haven't learned to handle emotions in these situations compassionately, we will most likely use anger, power, or shame instead.

If you think about how people handle their emotions in our world today, it becomes clear that some people can be compassionate with themselves and others, and some just don't have that ability.

Any adult can learn how to be compassionate, but we must learn self-compassion for our mistakes before we will have the energy or ability to be compassionate with others about their mistakes, especially our children.

Imagine looking at the world around you and seeing more compassionate responses. How do you envision that? What would look different? In my case, I watch what happens to people when they learn to have compassion for themselves through the therapy process. I watch how they learn to take life's falls as opportunities for growth, rather than confirmation of their inadequacies.

As small children, interpreting the infinite number of interactions in our car, we may, because of our immature thinking, come to believe that we're not good enough or not something enough.

But when we come to understand that life is hard and that no matter how good we are, we're still going to fall, our worthiness is no longer something we're searching for or proving every day. When we walk into the bakery and the clerk is mean to us, we can understand that they are having a bad day rather than letting it affect our self-esteem.

When my husband is in a really grumpy mood, I can use self-compassion and remind myself that my husband is not my mother, and I am okay; he just didn't get a good night's sleep.

If you grew up with a non-compassionate parent, it's likely that when you interact with people who have a similar tone, you will have to work hard not to be hurt by it.

You're okay. You're brave to have read this. Hopefully, whatever you discovered will be a light in your life. You may also be thinking that this is for and about other people, not you, but I really *am* saying it to *you*, because every human is enough and okay. The more you come to grips with your okay-ness, the less of your precious, valuable life energy you'll spend trying to prove it.

When you're no longer interested in proving that you are worthy or valuable, all that energy goes to making the world a safer, more loving, more connected place for every one of us.

Notes

_____

_____

_____

_____

_____

_____

_____

_____

_____

_____

_____

_____

_____

_____

_____

_____

_____

_____

_____

_____

7
Driving Forward

Our roles in our cars last a lifetime; in many ways, I will always be the lonely little girl in the back seat. Regardless of the fact that I am a parent, a grandparent, a professor, and a therapist, that little girl is still very much alive in me, in the stories in my head that tell me I don't matter and am not good enough. With my clients, I refer to their adult achievements as substantiating evidence that their childhood role may be a part of a much larger and more empowering mosaic that represents them. I know that I am also all of those things, but my inner hurt little girl still needs compassion.

Our roles may be challenged by life's circumstances. In my case, after my mother died, I was the sole caregiver for my aging father for nine years. During that time, our roles shifted dramatically as happens for many families with aging parents. My father, who had always been in the driver's seat in our car, had to learn to be a passenger as his ability to operate a motor vehicle declined. Some older adults begin to feel uncomfortable in the driver's seat and, literally and figuratively, give up the keys.

My father was not a willing participant in the transfer of the keys and was angry, blaming me during the last years of his life for taking away his independence. It is true; I did that. My intent was to keep him (and others) safe, but he felt like he was nothing if he was not the driver. I understood that, but his repeated criticism of me still cut me deeply, as it always had. Even though I was now driving the car, I felt as lonely and unseen as I always had. But I could feel lonely and unseen and still feel compassion for myself and for his loss of being the driver.

The additional roles we acquire as adults may be diverse and seemingly incongruous with our childhood roles. I see them as points of light that form through the integration of hard work and perseverance—all despite sometimes feeling hopeless and powerless in our human experiences.

My wish for the readers of this book is that you make peace with your childhood roles. Identify them and acknowledge the gifts and the losses that came with them. Give yourself the compassion you deserved. Try to gain a compassionate understanding of your sibling's roles, as they were only trying to matter in your car. Create the next generation of cars in your family, ones that will honor the light of each child inside them.

How do you do that?

You've already taken the first step: understanding how your family shaped you.

The second step is to expand your vision of yourself. We are each a work in progress. As we grow and learn, we expand and deepen, developing qualities we may not have had when we formed our view of ourselves. Ask yourself:

- Am I creative?
- Am I intuitive?
- Am I persistent?

- Am I resilient?
- Am I open?
- Am I assertive?
- Am I capable?
- Am I caring?
- Am I hopeful?
- Am I optimistic?
- Am I vulnerable?
- Am I hard-working?
- Have I shown bravery?
- Have I shown tolerance?
- Have I shown leadership?
- What other qualities have I developed over my lifetime?

The third step is to act with intention—to act in accordance with this bigger picture of yourself, the fully-realized adult you have become as you have grown beyond the role you once had in your childhood car.

Maybe you were timid or fearful as a child and always saw yourself that way. If you realize that as an adult, you have done things that required bravery, you can start to see yourself as a person who is capable of bravery and act from that new understanding of yourself.

Going forward in your life, acknowledging the qualities you have developed as an adult will help you see yourself as more than who you learned you were in your family car. It will help you have compassion for the child you were and for yourself as an adult who is still learning and growing. And from that compassion for ourselves springs compassion for our parents, our siblings, our spouses, our children, our friends, our neighbors and coworkers and even strangers. Everyone travelled through their childhood in a family car, and everyone is learning and growing.

I hope the ideas and information in this book have given you insight into your life in a way that is powerful and affirming. I know it may have raised as many questions for you as answers, and it certainly may have uncovered a lot of feelings. You may feel quite comfortable with the journey this book has taken you on, or you may feel there's further to go and want to continue.

I believe that the journey of self-knowledge and awareness lasts a lifetime. At times, it helps to talk it through with a trusted person and at others, it helps to allow ourselves to sit and wonder. In any case, I hope the journey helps you find acceptance and peace.

Notes

_____

_____

_____

_____

_____

_____

_____

_____

_____

_____

_____

_____

_____

_____

_____

_____

_____

_____

_____

_____

_____

_____

_____

Acknowledgments

In one particular course I taught at the University of Michigan School of Social Work, the final class of the semester focused on working with couples. For this final class, my husband Paul would participate in an activity where we played ourselves as a real couple and talked about a problem that we wanted the class to help us with as they were learning to be therapists.

We did this exercise together every semester, and each time, we talked in the car on the way to Ann Arbor about what problem we would discuss. This was tricky because we wanted to be authentic while still retaining healthy boundaries. Invariably, we decided to talk about the problem that Paul wanted me to write a book and I didn't want to do it. Each time, the class would explore why I didn't want to do it and how Paul could deal with that.

My reasons were centered on wanting to deliver my thoughts and insights in person with people; I couldn't imagine putting them on a written page and not being with a person when they read them. After one of these sessions, a couple of students came up to me after class and asked if I had ever thought of doing a podcast. I wasn't exactly sure what that was, but the student was insistent that her fiancé was a news broadcaster and could help me create one. That news broadcaster was Tolly Taylor, who eventually hosted my first six podcasts and sent me on my journey. Thank you to Bethany, Tolly's wife, for believing in my skills. Thank you to the hundreds of students who learned from me, many of whom are still a part of my life.

This book exists because of Beth Robinson. Beth is a writer who understood the concepts of the family car and helped me express them in a coherent, thoughtful, and cohesive way. I would still be wordsmithing the first chapter without her. She led me through the writing, editing, and publishing of this book. I depended on her encouragement, insistence, and hopefulness to follow through with this process.

I would like to thank my clients. It is an honor to be a witness to your lives, and your stories are reflected in the concepts of this book.

About the Author

Ellen Yashinsky Chute, LMSW, ACSW is a clinical social worker, consultant, mental health educator, and former adjunct lecturer at the University of Michigan School of Social Work. She has dedicated three decades to helping individuals, families, and teams realize and reach their potential. As a practitioner and educator, she has focused on trauma, social work ethics, relationships, family development, domestic abuse, and divorce. Ellen lives in Michigan with her husband Paul. *What Drives You* is her first book.

Bibliography

Bigler, J.J., Wetchler, J.L. (2015). *Handbook of LGBT-affirmative couple and family therapy*. Routledge.

Brach, T. (2019). *Radical compassion: Learning to love yourself and your world with the practice of RAIN*. Penguin Books

Brown, B. (2015). *Rising strong: How the ability to reset transforms the way we live, love, parent, and lead*. Spiegel and Grau.

Brown, B. (2021). *Atlas of the heart: Mapping meaningful connection and the language of human experience*. Random House.

Davies, D., Troy, M.F. (2015). *Child development: A practitioner's guide*. Guilford Press.

Duquette, P. (1997). The role of the real relationship in long term psychotherapy. *International Journal of Psychotherapy and Critical Thought*, 4(1), 11-20.

Felitti, V., Anda, R., Nordenberg, D., Williamson, D., Spitz, A., Edwards, V., Koss, M., Marks, J. (1998). Relationship of childhood abuse and household dysfunction to many of the leading causes of death in adults: The adverse childhood experiences (ACE) study. *American Journal of Preventive Medicine*, 14(4), 245-258.

Gilbert, R.M. (2004). *The eight concepts of Bowen theory: A new way of thinking about the individual and the group*. Leading Systems Press.

Gottman, J., Silver, N. (1994). *Why marriages succeed or fail: And how you can make yours last*. Simon and Schuster.

Herman, J.L. (1997). *Trauma and recovery: The aftermath of violence*. Basic Books.

Katz, J. (2006). *The macho paradox: Why some men hurt women and how all men can help*. Source Books.

Linehan, Marsha M. (1993). *Skills training manual for treating borderline personality disorder*. Guilford Press.

Perel, E. (2017). *The state of affairs: Rethinking infidelity*. Harper.

Perry, B.D., Winfrey, O. (2021). *What happened to you?: Conversations on trauma, resilience, and healing*. Flatiron Books.

Prochaska, J.O., Norcross, J.C., DiClemente, C. (1994). *Changing for good: A revolutionary six-stage program for overcoming bad habits and moving your life positively forward*. Quill.

McGoldrick, M., Hardy, K.V. (2019). *Re-visioning family therapy: Race, culture, and gender in clinical practice*. Guilford Press.

McGoldrick, M., Giordano, J., Garcia-Preto, N. (1994). *Ethnicity and family therapy*. Guilford Press.

McGoldrick, M., Gerson, R., Petry, S. (1985). *Genograms: Assessment and intervention*. Guilford Press.

Real, T. (1997). *I don't want to talk about it: Overcoming the secret legacy of male depression*. Scribners.

Scarf, M. (1995). *Intimate worlds: How families thrive and why they fail*. Random House.

Schnarch, D. (1997). *Passionate marriage: Keeping love and intimacy alive in committed relationships*. W.W. Norton & Company.

Schore, A.N. (2003). *Affect regulation and the repair of the self*. W.W. Norton & Company.

Schwartz, R.C. (1995). *Internal family systems therapy*. Guilford Press.

Shapiro, F. (2013). *Getting past your past: Take control of your life with self-help techniques from EMDR therapy*. Rodale Books.

Siegel, D. (2017). *Mind: A journey to the heart of being human*. W.W. Norton & Company.

Stosny, S. (2003). *Manual of the core value workshop*. Booksurge, LLC.

Tronick. E. (2007). *The neurobehavioral and social-emotional development of infants and children*. W.W. Norton & Company.

van der Kolk, B.A., McFarlane, A.C., & Weisath, L., eds. (1996). *Traumatic stress: The overwhelming experience on mind, body, and society*. Guilford Press.

van der Kolk, B.A. (2014). *The body keeps the score: Brain, mind, and body in the healing of trauma*. Viking Penguin.

CPSIA information can be obtained
at www.ICGtesting.com
Printed in the USA
LVHW112023010622
720195LV00017B/1497